FRANCIS FRITH'S
DAVENTRY
LIVING MEMORIES

ANGELA AND DAVID ADAMS have lived in Daventry for the last eighteen years, although it was about forty years ago that David met and married locally born Angela in Daventry. David had come to Daventry from Colchester as a trainee BBC engineer. Following early retirement from the BBC, David is now the House Steward at Canons Ashby House, a National Trust property, and lectures for the Workers Education Association in Architectural History and Collection Management. Angela had always worked in libraries until ten years ago, but latterly she has worked in museums. She is currently working at Rugby School Museum, and is also an active volunteer at Canons Ashby. Until recently, David and Angela were respectively Chairman and Secretary of the Friends of Daventry Museum.

FRANCIS FRITH'S
PHOTOGRAPHIC MEMORIES

DAVENTRY
LIVING MEMORIES

ANGELA AND
DAVID ADAMS

First published in the United Kingdom in 2005

Hardback Edition Published in 2005 ISBN 1-84589-006-X

Paperback Edition 2005 ISBN 1-85937-670-3

British Library Cataloguing in Publication Data

Daventry Living Memories
Angela and David Adams

The Francis Frith Collection
Frith's Barn, Teffont,
Salisbury, Wiltshire SP3 5QP
Tel: +44 (0) 1722 716 376
Email: info@francisfrith.co.uk
www.francisfrith.co.uk

Printed and bound in Great Britain

Front Cover: **DAVENTRY,** *High Street c1965* D83070t
Frontispiece: **BRAUNSTON,** *The Marina c1965* B778015

*The colour-tinting is for illustrative purposes only, and is not intended
to be historically accurate*

Aerial photographs reproduced under licence from
Simmons Aerofilms Limited.
Historical Ordnance Survey maps reproduced under licence from
Homecheck.co.uk
Every attempt has been made to contact copyright holders of
illustrative material. We will be happy to give full
acknowledgement in future editions for any items not credited.
Any information should be directed to The Francis Frith Collection.

AS WITH ANY HISTORICAL DATABASE THE FRITH ARCHIVE IS
CONSTANTLY BEING CORRECTED AND IMPROVED AND THE
PUBLISHERS WOULD WELCOME INFORMATION ON OMISSIONS OR
INACCURACIES

CONTENTS

Angela & David Adams would like to acknowledge all the help that has been given to them in the research and preparation for this book. Friends and fellow Daventrians have evoked many memories for them and have raised many questions, which they have yet to answer. One day - maybe!

ACKNOWLEDGEMENTS

Jeanette & Barry Adams

George Atkinson

Julia Barry

Margaret & Ian Boughton

Shirley Carwardine

Kay Clarke

Betty Cox

Ethel Crankshaw

Patrick Crecraft

Richard Dibben

Pam Emery

Helen & Ray Goddard

Alf Goodridge

Barbara Gray

Rowena Haigh

Doris Hughes

Janet & Stephen Hupfield

Sheila Hupfield

Hazel & Norman Jones

Marcus Lewis

Stan Nicholls

Marian Orgill

Elizabeth Powell

Dawn Quinn

Gwen Rintoul

Stan Ruddlestone

Mike Rumbold

Roy & Ted Sharpe

Derek Smith

Mez & Mike Tebbitt

Joan Turley

Gordon Turner

Dave Warner

Peter Wagstaffe

Rev Kenneth Ward

Sue Yates

FRANCIS FRITH
VICTORIAN PIONEER

FRANCIS FRITH, founder of the world-famous photographic archive, was a complex and multi-talented man. A devout Quaker and a highly successful Victorian businessman, he was philosophical by nature and pioneering in outlook.

By 1855 he had already established a wholesale grocery business in Liverpool, and sold it for the astonishing sum of £200,000, which is the equivalent today of over £15,000,000. Now a very rich man, he was able to indulge his passion for travel. As a child he had pored over travel books written by early explorers, and his fancy and imagination had been stirred by family holidays to the sublime mountain regions of Wales and Scotland. 'What lands of spirit-stirring and enriching scenes and places!' he had written. He was to return to these scenes of grandeur in later years to 'recapture the thousands of vivid and tender memories', but with a different purpose. Now in his thirties, and captivated by the new science of photography, Frith set out on a series of pioneering journeys up the Nile and to the Near East that occupied him from 1856 unti 1860.

INTRIGUE AND EXPLORATION

These far-flung journeys were packed with intrigue and adventure. In his life story, written when he was sixty-three, Frith tells of being held captive by bandits, and of fighting 'an awful midnight battle to the very point of surrender with a deadly pack of hungry, wild dogs'. Wearing flowing Arab costume, Frith arrived at Akaba by camel sixty years before Lawrence of Arabia, where he encountered 'desert princes and rival sheikhs, blazing with jewel-hilted swords'.

He was the first photographer to venture beyond the sixth cataract of the Nile. Africa was still the mysterious 'Dark Continent', and Stanley and Livingstone's historic meeting was a decade into the future. The conditions for picture taking confound belief. He laboured for hours in his wicker darkroom in the sweltering heat of the desert, while the volatile chemicals fizzed dangerously in their trays. Back in London he exhibited his photographs and was 'rapturously cheered' by members of the Royal Society. His reputation as a photographer was made overnight.

VENTURE OF A LIFE-TIME

Characteristically, Frith quickly spotted the opportunity to create a new business as a specialist publisher of photographs. He lived in an era of immense and sometimes violent change. For the poor in the early part of Victoria's reign work was exhausting and the hours long, and people had precious little free time to enjoy themselves. Most people had no transport other than a cart or gig at their disposal, and rarely

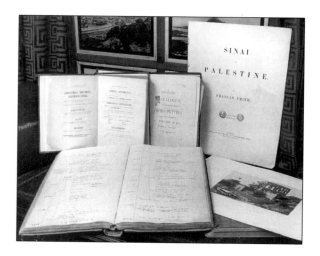

Frith's business one only has to look at the catalogue issued by Frith & Co in 1886: it runs to some 670 pages, listing not only many thousands of views of the British Isles but also many photographs of most European countries, and China, Japan, the USA and Canada - note the sample page shown on page 9 from the hand-written Frith & Co ledgers recording the pictures. By 1890 Frith had created the greatest specialist photographic publishing company in the world, with over 2,000 sales outlets - more than the combined number that Boots and WH Smith have today! The picture on the next page shows the Frith & Co display board at Ingleton in the Yorkshire Dales (left of window). Beautifully constructed with a mahogany frame and gilt inserts, it could display up to a dozen local scenes.

travelled far beyond the boundaries of their own town or village. However, by the 1870s the railways had threaded their way across the country, and Bank Holidays and half-day Saturdays had been made obligatory by Act of Parliament. All of a sudden the working man and his family were able to enjoy days out and see a little more of the world.

With typical business acumen, Francis Frith foresaw that these new tourists would enjoy having souvenirs to commemorate their days out. In 1860 he married Mary Ann Rosling and set out on a new career: his aim was to photograph every city, town and village in Britain. For the next thirty years he travelled the country by train and by pony and trap, producing fine photographs of seaside resorts and beauty spots that were keenly bought by millions of Victorians. These prints were painstakingly pasted into family albums and pored over during the dark nights of winter, rekindling precious memories of summer excursions.

THE RISE OF FRITH & CO

Frith's studio was soon supplying retail shops all over the country. To meet the demand he gathered about him a small team of photographers, and published the work of independent artist-photographers of the calibre of Roger Fenton and Francis Bedford. In order to gain some understanding of the scale of

POSTCARD BONANZA

The ever-popular holiday postcard we know today took many years to develop. In 1870 the Post Office issued the first plain cards, with a pre-printed stamp on one face. In 1894 they allowed other publishers' cards to be sent through the mail with an attached adhesive halfpenny stamp. Demand grew rapidly, and in 1895 a new size of postcard was permitted called the court card, but there was little room for illustration. In 1899, a year after Frith's death, a new card measuring 5.5 x 3.5 inches became the standard format, but it was not until 1902 that the divided back came into being, so that the address and message could be on one face and a full-size illustration on the other. Frith & Co were in the vanguard of postcard development: Frith's sons Eustace and Cyril continued their father's monumental task, expanding the number of views offered to the public and recording more and more places in Britain, as the coasts and countryside were opened up to mass travel.

Francis Frith had died in 1898 at his villa in Cannes, his great project still growing. The archive he created continued in business for another seventy years. By 1970 it contained over a third of a million pictures showing 7,000 British towns and villages.

FRANCIS FRITH'S LEGACY

Frith's legacy to us today is of immense significance and value, for the magnificent archive of evocative photographs he created provides a unique record of change in the cities, towns and villages throughout Britain over a century and more. Frith and his fellow studio photographers revisited locations many times down the years to update their views, compiling for us an enthralling and colourful pageant of British life and character.

We are fortunate that Frith was dedicated to recording the minutiae of everyday life, for it is this sheer wealth of visual data, the painstaking chronicle of changes in dress, transport, street layouts, buildings, housing, engineering and landscape that captivates us so much today. His remarkable images offer us a powerful link with the past and with the lives of our ancestors.

THE VALUE OF THE ARCHIVE TODAY

Computers have now made it possible for Frith's many thousands of images to be accessed almost instantly. Frith's images are increasingly used as visual resources, by social historians, by researchers into genealogy and ancestry, by architects and town planners, and by teachers involved in local history projects.

In addition, the archive offers every one of us an opportunity to examine the places where we and our families have lived and worked down the years. Highly successful in Frith's own era, the archive is now, a century and more on, entering a new phase of popularity. Historians consider the Francis Frith Collection to be of prime national importance. It is the only archive of its kind remaining in private ownership. Francis Frith's archive is now housed in an historic timber barn in the beautiful village of Teffont in Wiltshire. Its founder would not recognize the archive office as it is today. In place of the many thousands of dusty boxes containing glass plate negatives and an all-pervading odour of photographic chemicals, there are now ranks of computer screens. He would be amazed to watch his images travelling round the world at unimaginable speeds through internet lines.

The archive's future is both bright and exciting. Francis Frith, with his unshakeable belief in making photographs available to the greatest number of people, would undoubtedly approve of what is being done today with his lifetime's work. His photographs depicting our shared past are now bringing pleasure and enlightenment to millions around the world a century and more after his death.

DAVENTRY
AN INTRODUCTION

DAVENTRY is a small market town located near the hypothetical centre of England, 70 miles north of London and 40 miles south of Birmingham. What makes the area unique is the 'land bridge'. In order to travel from north to south in England without crossing a river, you will pass through an area where rivers rise and flow to the east and west. The River Nene rises here and flows to the Wash, the River Leam and the River Avon flow west to the Bristol Channel, while the River Cherwell wends its way south via Oxford to the Thames and the North Sea. Consequently this small area has always attracted long-distance travellers. The Romans built Watling Street, which runs 3 miles east of Daventry on its way to Anglesey. Until recently, Watling Street was still a main artery of the road network; it was turnpiked in the 18th century and classified as the A5 in the early 20th century. Canal builders also chose to follow this route, and there are major canal

BRAUNSTON, *The Canal c1965* B778014

junctions here at Norton and Braunston, allowing access to Oxford, Stratford, Birmingham, Leicester, and of course London. Now largely a major leisure facility, it was the backbone of Midlands industry until it was superseded by the railways. They in their turn also pass through this narrow corridor. Gone now are the days of the Night Mail 'crossing the border, bringing the cheque and the postal order', to quote from the famous poem by W H Auden, brilliantly transferred to film in the 1930s. The replacement is the M1, opened in the early 1960s, which sprang the village of Watford into the national vocabulary as a new north-south divide emerged, and 'South of Watford' became 'South of Watford Gap'!

Initially the area was inhabited by Stone Age people and Iron Age tribes, who built a fort larger than Maiden Castle on top of Borough Hill immediately to the east of Daventry; it is some 650 feet above sea-level, giving commanding views of the countryside. Only two miles to the south-west is Arbury Hill, the county's highest point at 734 feet, with its own Iron Age fort. When the Romans arrived, they in their turn fortified Borough Hill. Watling Street passes Daventry some three miles to the east, punctuated at Whilton Locks by the now lost Roman town of Bannaventa. The Roman army, however, chose to remain on Borough Hill to keep watch over the area.

The town of Daventry itself emerged through the Dark Ages under the Danelaw, and burgeoned as a market town once King Alfred drove the Danes back to the sea in the ninth century. Its name, 'Daventre' in the Middle Ages, is thought to mean 'Daffa's tree'. This might have been misread from a medieval document as 'Danetre' and related to a tree on Borough Hill, the Dane Tree where the Danes' moot or court was held.

Following the Norman invasion of 1066, Daventry continued to grow. In the 12th century, the Priory of St Augustine was founded in Daventry, and it survived almost until the Dissolution of the Monasteries. Because the monks refused to comply with Cardinal Wolsey's request for money to build his new Cardinals College in Oxford, he dissolved the foundation in 1526. There is no trace of this foundation left apart from a seal of Prior Nicholas found in the churchyard in the 18th century, and recently purchased by the Daventry District Council. The seal was until recently on display in the museum.

Daventry has often been in the news for one reason or another. The Civil War is a case in point: Charles I stayed in Daventry at the Wheatsheaf Hotel before his disastrous battle at Naseby in 1645. His army was encamped on Borough Hill.

As the 18th century unrolled, Watling Street was made into a turnpike. However, at Weedon the turnpike bore left up Weedon Hill and through Daventry, rejoining the Roman road somewhere north of Coventry. The resulting coach traffic, which rose at times to 80 coaches a day, brought prosperity to Daventry with the building of many coaching inns and the rise of a lucrative trade in making whips for the coachmen. Many of these inns have now closed or have been demolished. The photographs in this book record some of them, but only two coaching inns are still in business. Both are in Brook Street, on the old London to Holyhead road. One is the Dun Cow, and is relatively unchanged by time. The other, opposite, is the Saracen's Head, now a pub and restaurant. One reason for the success of the whip trade was Northamptonshire's long association with leather. It has always been a largely pastoral farming area, and the abundance of hides led to the leather trade being an important part of the county's economy. As the railways superseded the coaches, the whip trade died out in Daventry, but it was replaced by a successful boot and shoe industry. The last shoe factory closed here only recently.

These prosperous periods left their mark on Daventry, as in 1752 the crumbling parish church, the remains of the priory, was rebuilt in the modern Palladian style - it is the only Georgian town church in the diocese. At the same time, the non-conformist congregations built their own chapels. Daventry is most unusual in that the Congregational Church, now the United Reformed Church, is older than the parish church by 30 years - it was built in 1723. From this period, there remains the Assembly Hall at the rear of the Saracen's Head, built for meetings and entertainments for the gentry when they moved into their town houses for the winter. In 1752 the Congregationalists moved the Doddridge Academy from Northampton to Daventry. One of the students transferred to Daventry was Joseph Priestley, who later became famous for his experi-

ments with oxygen and who laid the foundations of the modern discipline of chemistry.

The 19th century and the burgeoning shoe trade saw new premises for the Methodists in 1824, who moved into New Street from their original chapel behind the Moot Hall, while in 1874 the Congregationalists added rooms to their chapel for the Sunday School. Meanwhile, in 1840, the Church of England built St James's Church for the increased population coming into Daventry to work in the shoe trade; many of these people were agricultural workers forced out of work by the enclosure of the old medieval open field systems.

The 20th century saw very different happenings thrusting Daventry into the homes of the world. In 1925 the BBC chose Borough Hill as the site for the their new national radio transmitter, which would bring a 'National' service to everyone in Britain from one site. This was followed in 1932 by the opening of the Empire Station, enabling George V to broadcast his Christmas message from Windsor Castle to the British Empire. Daventry continued to broadcast to the world until 1992, when the

DAVENTRY, *From Newnham Hill c1965* D83055

facility was transferred to other BBC World Service sites. Such was the power of the services radiated from here that many Daventry people reminisce about hearing the General Overseas Service's signature tune, 'Lillibullero', on their kettles and toasters! Experiments were conducted near Weedon in the 1930s using these services to prove the theory of Radar, an invention that is vital to the functioning of the world today. During this period there were other services using Borough Hill, including transmissions during the Second World War to aid the RAF to return to England from their missions over Germany.

Following the World Wars, with the birth of the new Elizabethan age of prosperity, a new major employer came to Daventry. In 1954 British Timken set up one of their European taper roller bearing factories here. (This factory has only recently closed - its site is now another housing estate). The 1960s heralded a new era of development and expansion, as Birmingham selected Daventry as a town to help house and employ their growing population. In 1967 the Ford Motor Company built a vast warehouse to house their International Distribution Centre. The small market town had a population of 5000; this was suddenly expanded to 20,000 by the 1990s, and is now projected to rise to over 40,000 by 2020. Needless to say, vast areas of countryside and farmland have been used for housing and industrial estates, and a new bypass and ring road has been constructed. We now have a reputation as 'the town with all the roundabouts'! The latest phase of this development is being carried out using plans drawn up with the help of the Civic Trust.

This book of photographs, which concentrates on the 1950s and 1960s, captures much of the charm of Daventry before its awakening to the pressures of modern life. The streets are remarkably quiet, and the established small shopkeepers are still supplying the needs of the residents. It would be interesting to see another book covering the last 30 years and to witness the differences that progress has made to this small medieval market town.

DAVENTRY, *Recreation Ground c1965* D83084

DAVENTRY *from the air 1928* AF24681c

THE MARKET PLACE AND ITS SURROUNDINGS

THE BURTON MEMORIAL
c1960 D83061

The tour starts with this excellent cameo shot which shows the heart and essence of Daventry, the Moot Hall, centre of local government during the 20th century, and the Burton Memorial, erected in 1907, celebrating the life of Edmund Charles Burton. He was a stalwart of 19th-century local government, being the third successive member of his family to be Town Clerk. A huntsman and churchman, according to the inscription he was 'Sans peur, sans reproche'. It was while the Burton family were in office that the old Moot Hall on the site of this memorial was demolished and the Town Council moved into the present Moot Hall.

THE MOOT HALL *c1950* D83001

This photograph, taken shortly after the war, shows the Moot Hall in a rather sorry state of repair. Northamptonshire sandstone is subject to severe weathering, and this photograph shows that time, money and man-power were not available to keep this façade in good order. The building at the extreme left of the picture, behind the porch, was the first Methodist chapel in the town; it was later used to house Daventry's fire engine. Outside the Moot Hall is an early concrete telephone box designed by Gilbert Scott.

▶ THE MOOT HALL *c1965* D83057

The Moot Hall has now been renovated, and looks worthy of its status as the Town Hall. This fine Georgian town house became the Moot Hall and residence of the Town Council around 1800. This role continued until the re-organisation of local government in 1972. With the formation of the Daventry District Council, the Charter Trustees were formed to look after Daventry's charters and town regalia. It was not until 2003 that a new Daventry Town Council was set up. By this time the Moot Hall was in use as a museum and Tourist Information Centre, with the Mayor's Parlour still operative on the top floor. It is sad that the building is at present empty, following the closure of the museum and TIC in 2004. The Town Council have moved to new premises in Bishop Crewe House, part of the old Grammar School.

THE BURTON MEMORIAL AND THE MOOT HALL *c1950* D83003

The Market Square is at the junction of the High Street, Abbey Street and Chapel Lane. Chapel Lane was formerly Hogmarket, and is now called St John's Place. The Plume of Feathers, the rendered building on the right, is shown on an earlier postcard by Rodhouse of Daventry as stone-built. The sign Maple Leaf Court is on the corner of the building known previously as the Peacock Hotel, but it was at this time divided into flats.

THE BURTON MEMORIAL AND THE MOOT HALL *c1965* D83044

In this photograph, taken from a similar viewpoint to D83003, the buildings in Chapel Lane have been demolished, opening up the view to Warden's Lodge, part of Daventry Grammar School. To the right is a bus standing in the Market Square, waiting to leave for Northampton. Just visible to the left is Gyte's fish and chip shop, which closed many years ago.

MARKET SQUARE
c1955 D83026

Comparing this with D83003, we see that the Plume of Feathers now has bow windows and has been repainted. Next door is a snack bar, which disappeared shortly after this photograph was taken. The buildings that run on down Abbey Street have long since been demolished and replaced by The Abbey Centre and a new leisure complex. The new road signs do little to enhance the charm of the area.

**MARKET SQUARE AND
THE BURTON MEMORIAL**
c1960 D83062

Here is a general view of
the old centre of Daventry.
Comparing this with
the earlier pictures, the
memorial has gained a
chequered kerbstone and
a rash of road signs. It is
looking sadly isolated,
especially now that the
backdrop of cottages
has disappeared. Today,
fortunately, the kerb and
road signs have gone,
and the road to the left is
pedestrianised, which has
reunited the memorial to its
surroundings. However, the
hub of the town has now
moved to Bowen Square, the
1970s shopping precinct.

21

► **MARKET SQUARE**
1964 D83050

This is similar to photograph D83062, page 21, and clearly shows some of the house clearances of the last ten years. The cottages down Abbey Street to the left of the memorial have gone, and the United Counties Bus Company now have a garage there. Similarly, the cottages on the Market Square have gone. Seckerson, the hairdresser's, has become 'Maison Seckerson, Hair Stylist'. This shop has had several uses since 1964, namely a solicitor's office, a small supermarket and currently a bathroom showroom.

◄ **MARKET SQUARE**
1964 D83045

Dumayne's second-hand furniture shop to the right (it was a snack bar in a previous picture) has had a modern shop front inserted. It was later used by the Council as their Treasurer's department; it was then demolished in the late 1980s to make way for the Abbey Centre, built to provide facilities for Daventry's care organisations.

▲ **THE ABBEY BUILDINGS** *c1950* D83005

To the south of the Market Square are the abbey buildings. This is a Victorian reconstruction of the last remnants of the Cluniac priory. Over the centuries it has been used as a school, a gaol and a poorhouse. The County Library was based here in the 1950s. It was opened twice a week by Mr Webb, the headmaster of the Abbey School - its sign with a flaming torch can be seen on the right-hand end of the building. A Coronation tea for children took place in the upstairs room in 1953 - the unusual treat of banana sandwiches was provided.

◄ **THE ABBEY BUILDINGS** *c1965* D83046

In the 1950s, part of the building was used as overflow classrooms for the Abbey School, which at that time provided all primary education for the town. The school can be seen on the left. It was also used for the Mother and Baby Clinic. The neighbouring Holy Cross church used it as their church rooms; breakfast would be served there on Sundays after the service in church. It is now used as the Daventry Ex-Servicemen's Club, after a brief period as a restaurant.

MARKET SQUARE
c1950 D83008

Market Square has some vehicles parked on it, including a Ralph Rossa ice cream van (right), from Leicester. The Ancient Order of Foresters Friendly Society is the building to the right of the church, which later became the Daventry Christian Assembly. The cottages on the left were demolished sometime in the 1960s. In the one that was double-fronted lived Mr and Mrs Terry. The cottages are currently being replaced - the price of progress! Regay the cleaners and dyers have their van parked outside their shop (left).

▲ **HOLY CROSS CHURCH** *c1965* D83069

This is a fine view of Holy Cross Church with
the Abbey Buildings on the left. The Ancient
Order of Foresters Friendly Society Institute is
on the right. These societies sprang up in the
19th century to help poorer families to save
for rainy days, and to help provide decent
burials for them. This building later became the
Daventry Christian Assembly, where Christians
who were not members of the town's churches
and chapels could meet together. It is now a
private house. The wall to its left, where the
girl is sitting, was the site of the Swan Inn, yet
another of Daventry's hostelries.

▲ HOLY CROSS CHURCH AND THE MARKET SQUARE *c1965* D83073

It is a busy day on the Market Square. The earliest recorded market in Daventry was in 1203, and this was formalised in the charters of 1576 and 1595. However, there was no market here in the 1940s or 1950s; the market was restarted in the late 1960s on the Market Square and transferred to the High Street around 1990, where it still operates on Tuesdays and Fridays.

HOLY CROSS CHURCH
c1955 D83017

Holy Cross Church is the only Georgian town church in Peterborough diocese. It was rebuilt in 1752 after the remnant of the Cluniac priory church became unsafe. Designed by William and David Hiorn of Warwick, the design is reminiscent of St Martin in the Fields, London, by James Gibb. He later designed All Saints, Derby, now Derby Cathedral. The Hiorn brothers worked as masons at Derby, and when they were approached by Daventry for a new church design, they used Derby as a model.

HOLY CROSS CHURCH, *The Interior c1955* D83018

If this photograph was put alongside one of Derby Cathedral, it would be obvious where the design originated. The over-large capitals to the columns are 'Chinese copies' of those in Derby. To the casual viewer, however, this interior view of Holy Cross church looks unchanged today, apart from the light fittings. However, redecoration was done in 1963, which restored the original colour scheme. The old Georgian box pews remain, though they were lowered in height in the 19th century. The Willis organ replaced the previous organ, which was destroyed by a fire in 1859 - the cause? The organ tuner's candle fell down inside the mechanism while he was tuning the organ!

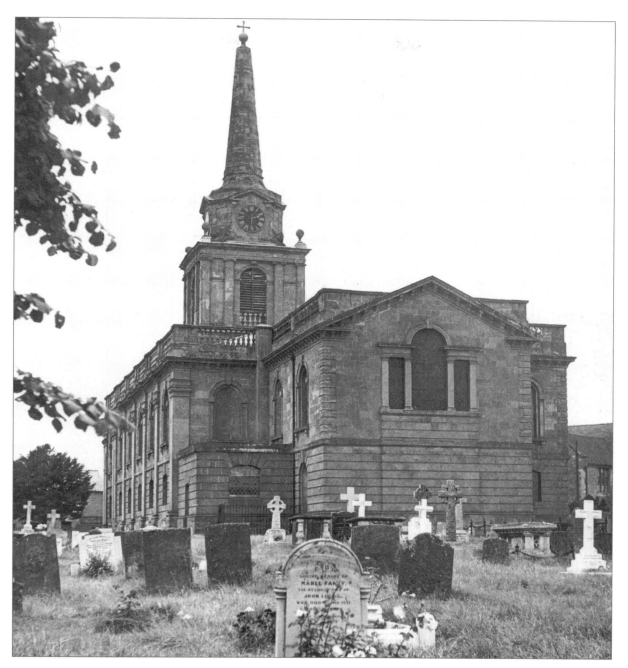

HOLY CROSS CHURCH *c1955* D83007

The churchyard in Daventry is reportedly one of the largest in the country, but is now closed for burials. Children from the Abbey School in the 1950s had to cross the churchyard to go to the canteen for school dinners - this had to be timed to avoid funerals. The eastern end of the church has a fine Venetian window, a typical feature of 18th-century Palladian architecture.

29

HIGH STREET AND NORTH STREET

THE BURTON MEMORIAL AND HIGH STREET *c1950* D83004

As we turn our back on the Market Square, High Street runs westward to Sheaf Street. This view shows Burton's memorial standing at the top of the High Street on the spot where the original Moot Hall stood in 1788. Behind it is Frost's, a tobacconist's and confectioner's, which was demolished in 1951. Danetre Café on the left, known as Leigh's, is where the Daventry Town Ladies Hockey Team had tea for 1s per person in the 1930s.

HIGH STREET
c1965 D83070

Looking along the High Street past the beleaguered Burton Memorial, one would see little change today in the buildingscape. Danetre Bakery (left) has long gone, and the building society on the extreme left in this photograph may be the old Anglian Building Society before they became the Nationwide and moved across the road. The Milk Bar (centre right), built in 1952, has replaced the tobacconists seen in picture D83004. It was a favourite meeting place for Grammar School pupils, and is still in business today. The adjacent Lion and Lamb, however, is now called Friday's.

HIGH STREET *c1950* D83002

The High Street is looking remarkably quiet and empty – there are only a few vans and cars, and no road markings. The upstairs bay window of the shop on the left is no longer to be seen, as the façade has been rebuilt. It belonged to Tower's, who were boot makers. The Lion & Lamb on the right displays the star trademark of the Northampton Brewery Company. This company amalgamated with Phipps, the other major brewer in Northampton. They in turn were taken over by the Watney Mann group in 1962.

▼ **HIGH STREET** *c1960* D83027

Another quiet day in the High Street; perhaps the photograph was taken on a Wednesday, which was early closing day. Most of the buildings are still recognisable, but only Lloyds Bank, now Lloyds TSB, is still trading. Lloyds' building was built for the old City and Counties bank, and the superb coat of arms sculpted on the side is plain to see. The three shops on the right, where the barber's pole is, were demolished in the 1970s to make the entrance to Bowen Square. The barbers were Messrs Bolton & Warne, with Bird's the greengrocer's this side and Walker's bakery on the other side.

▶ **HIGH STREET**

c1965 D83053

The Working Mens' Club is receiving a lick of paint. The Working Men's Club is now at The Lodge, Welton Road, just out of sight to the left down Abbey Street. On the left is the Trustee Savings Bank, which had just opened in Daventry with Barbara Green as their first cashier. The bank encouraged young savers by providing services in the lunch hour at the Grammar School. The TSB was absorbed by Lloyds Bank, which in Daventry just happened to be next door!

HIGH STREET *c1965*
D83049

Comparing this to picture D83053, we can see that the decorators have changed position. The painter is now 'footing' the ladder for his colleague. This picture clearly shows Lloyds Bank as the neighbour of the TSB. Just further on across North Street, the new building is Newman's, the first supermarket-style shop to open in Daventry. It is now the offices of the Nationwide Building Society.

▶ **THE GRAMMAR SCHOOL**
c1965 D83020

North Street joins High Street by Lloyds Bank, and it is down here on the left that we find the last Daventry Grammar School building. The Grammar School was founded in 1576 by William Parker, a Daventrian who became a wealthy merchant in London. The school was originally situated in New Street. This photograph shows the later building, built in 1937, which itself became redundant following the amalgamation of the Grammar School and the Secondary Modern School in the 1980s. That school on Ashby Road is now known as William Parker School. This building at present houses the County Library, but redevelopment plans are afoot!

HIGH STREET

c1950 D83009

Judging by the clothes worn by the two ladies on the right, it is thought that this photograph was taken in the late 1940s. They are passing two of the main food shops of the town. On the extreme right is the Co-op butcher, whose meat won many prizes, and next door is Golding & Son, a grocer, whose shop was renowned for the smell of good coffee. The Rugby Provident Building Society on the left became part of the Hinckley & Rugby Building Society in 1983.

35

▼ **NORTH STREET** *c1965* D83029

The attractive Beehive Cottage on the right was originally the lodge to Captain Stopford's house on Ashby Road. That house, alas, was demolished, and the site used to build the Community Centre. For many years Grammar School pupils used North Street to reach their sports ground at the bottom of the hill. We now return up the hill to High Street.

▶ **HIGH STREET**
c1965 D83078

Daventry High Street is now looking very busy. The Co-op have modernised their premises from the original three shops (a baker's, a grocer's and a butcher's) to a modern supermarket. Golding & Son, the grocer's beyond, has been replaced by Rainbow's carpet shop. The white building to the right of the Co-op still houses the Conservative Club. On the left, Jean Green has opened her fashion shop, bringing style to the ladies of the town.

◀ **HIGH STREET** *c1955*
D83028

The two impressive buildings to the right now house the Natwest Bank, previously the National Provincial and originally the Northamptonshire Union Bank. Rodhouse's, a milliner's and draper's (extreme right), are still remembered with much affection in the town by the many ladies who bought their hats and bonnets there, made by the Misses Rodhouse.

▶ **HIGH STREET**
c1948 D83011

The car on the left obscures what was the front window of the Daventry Weekly Express office (or The Gusher, as it is affectionately known by the locals). In 1981 they crossed the road to the building occupied here by E Harris, the chemist (second from the right). On the extreme right is Wood Bros, wine merchants, and above the shop there were two flats, both rented at one time by BBC trainee engineers and their families. This building, a fine example of a Georgian town house, is now Barclays Bank.

HIGH STREET *c1948*
D83010

This view of the High Street shows many buildings that have either since disappeared or have been radically reworked. The gable-ended house at the centre of the picture at the end of the High Street was demolished when Tavern Lane was widened in about 1955. The first building on the left, and the second, Maloney & Sons, jewellers, were demolished to make a new entrance to Foundry Place in the late 1960s. Further on, on the left, hoardings around the Midland Bank suggest that this photograph might have been taken in 1948, just before the bank opened. The Northamptonshire Farmers building on the right was demolished and rebuilt as a supermarket. It is now the Argos store.

▶ **HIGH STREET** *c1965*
D83075

Paynes, a shoe repairer's, and Nan Barton the florist (right) are no longer, and nor is Hargrave's beyond, a butcher's. In this area there is now a building society, estate agent and a charity shop. How times have changed! The new brick building (centre right) is George Mason's, one of the early supermarkets in Daventry. In contrast, however, Howkins, Staite & Sons, estate agents (second left) have closed their office here, though half is still occupied by Taylor's Estate Agency.

HIGH STREET

c1965 D83077

The Victorian Jacobethan-style house facing up the High Street was the BBC club for many years. The seven-bay stone Georgian town house on the left was in part the Mid Northants Water Board offices for many years. By this time Baxters, the butchers, had replaced part of the façade, but today two more modern shop fronts fill it. Willoughby's (next to Baxter's) was the leading shoe shop in Daventry; today it is another estate agent's office. The building to left, which was Moloney's the jewellers, was demolished in the 1970s to make a new entrance through to the Bowen Square shopping precinct via Foundry Place.

▲ **HIGH STREET** *c1965* D83064

Looking down the High Street we can see Fosters Brothers (centre right) in a new building that replaced the Bear Hotel, one of Daventry's coaching inns. Babyland beyond was the new name for Trinder's shops - they sold not only prams, but also bicycles. Northamptonshire Farmers Ltd (right) was a form of co-operative for the farmers for supplies for their farms. It also supplied food and accessories for pet owners in the town. For many years Mr Hiscox was the manager and Jim Chapman a loyal employee. The building was replaced during redevelopment, and Argos now trade there.

HIGH STREET
c1965 D83065

In this view the family businesses of Hargrave's the butcher's (right) and Trott's the greengrocer's next door are still in business, though not for much longer. Trott's closed in 1968, and is at present a mobile phone shop. Collett's, the women's outfitter, has closed, as we can see from the boarded up window on the extreme left; this is now a charity shop. Barclays Bank (next to Trott's) arrived in Daventry in the 1960s to replace Wood Bros, wine and spirit merchants.

DAVENTRY *from the air 1967* AFA177020

SHEAF STREET AND LONDON ROAD

SHEAF STREET *c1950* D83012

We now turn left from the High Street into Sheaf Street and look back down the hill to Brook Street. The scene appears very quiet, with only one car and a cyclist to be seen. This street was the original London to Holyhead turnpike, and along it stood twelve hostelries providing for the passing trade of up to 80 coaches a day. The World's End, a Phipps's house, was one of these pubs (second right). Brook Street also had at least four pubs as well. Up until about 1960 Sheaf Street still had two-way traffic, with double-decker buses precariously carrying their passengers up and down it.

SHEAF STREET
c1965 D83066

Redevelopment of Daventry began in the early sixties under a scheme to house Birmingham overspill population. The Daventry Civic Society was formed to preserve this historic street from demolition. Many of the properties were in need of restoration, but fortunately they were saved. Today the street is looking much smarter, and has also been pedestrianised. Brook Street, however, was largely demolished, as we can see from the void in the distance.

SHEAF STREET *c1950* D83022

The Marquis of Granby was another one of the many pubs and alehouses in the town centre that no longer exist. The building to the left of it was for many years a printer's and stationer's and the original offices of the Daventry Express. Many of these buildings have been demolished to make way for Foundry Walk and the post office. The building with the lady leaning out of the window (six buildings from the right) is still standing; it housed the post office until 1963, when the present post office opened.

THE WHEAT SHEAF HOTEL
c1950 D83021

This old coaching inn is one of many in Daventry which stood on the London to Holyhead turnpike. Founded in 1610, it is reputed to be the place where Charles I stayed before the Battle of Naseby in 1645. It is now a nursing home for the elderly. The monkey-puzzle tree, which still stands, has fascinated generations of children. It is interesting to note that the signwriter who worked on the wall to the left must have kept his eyes on his job - if he had looked up he would have noticed there should be a space in Wheat Sheaf!

LONDON ROAD *c1955* D83023

London Road, as the name implies, was the turnpike from London; it climbs up to the Wheat Sheaf, one of several coaching inns in Daventry. The coaching trade caused Daventry to become a leading centre for the manufacture of whips. It is believed that the tall Wellingtonia trees on the right-hand side of the road were planted to commemorate the birth of the children of the Burton family. It is a member of the same family that is commemorated by the Burton Memorial.

LONDON ROAD
c1955 D83024

Looking south along London Road, we see several of the desirable bungalows and villas built by Messrs Bosworth & Wakeford, many of which are still owned by them. This main thoroughfare was by-passed in the 1930s, bringing a little calm to this approach to the town centre.

DANETRE HOSPITAL *c1965* D83067

This fine ivy-clad building was new in 1834, when it was opened as the Union Workhouse for the area. After the Workhouse closed, it was used as a geriatric hospital. Unfortunately, until recently, many of the old people in Daventry had a fear of 'ending up in the workhouse' as they became infirm. A new hospital is currently being built behind this wonderful 19th-century façade.

NEW STREET AND THE 'REC'

THE POLICE STATION *c1965* D83080

We return up London Road to the Wheat Sheaf and turn right into New Street, formerly called Lichfield Street, which takes us back to the Market Place. Around 1960 redevelopment started in New Street with the demolition of the old police station. This view shows its replacement in the functional style of the day. It was extended in 1995 to cope with the increase in population. The stone building to the right is the Magistrates' Courthouse, also built around 1960.

THE RECREATION GROUND
c1965 D83083

The Recreation Ground, known as 'the Rec', was purchased by public subscription started in 1887, the year of Queen Victoria's Golden Jubilee. It was presented to the town for the people in 1892. This view shows the play area, with the 'Witch's Hat' to the left of the roundabout. The scene is backed by the then new police station.

THE RECREATION GROUND *c1965* D83084

This view of the Rec shows the steam engine hiding the terrace of houses known as Mount Pleasant. The building on the extreme left is Stead & Simpson's shoe factory, one of the last shoe manufacturers to survive in Daventry, once home to many factories and craftsman. Steads's factory has now disappeared, to be replaced by Tesco's supermarket and obligatory car park. Fortunately, the Rec still survives.

THE RECREATION GROUND
c1965 D83085

This steam engine spent its working life in Byfield stone quarry until it closed in 1965. It was then moved to the Rec, and became a great attraction for the local children. It has recently been removed, largely because of Health and Safety considerations. In the background is the spire of Holy Cross Church. The building in front of that was the Methodist Church from 1824 until they moved to their new building in Lodge Road in 1974. The old building, rather ironically, is now Freddie's Pub.

51

NEW STREET

c1965 D83043

Looking down New Street to the Moot Hall, we can see on the right a brick Georgian house where many BBC trainees lodged in the 1960s. It is now offices of the Rider Charity, who supply motorcycles for medical staff in Africa. The building next door with the central archway was a timber workshop which Jan Hupfield (née Lodge) remembers visiting regularly to collect sawdust for her pet mice.

53

OUTER DAVENTRY AND PANORAMAS

HEMANS ROAD *c1965* D83038

DRYDEN AVENUE *c1965* D83039

TENNYSON ROAD
c1965 D83040

SHAKESPEARE AVENUE *c1965* D83041

Having completed the tour of Daventry town centre, we now look at some of the 20th-century housing and industrial development. This group of four photographs of the council estate show it soon after it was built in the late 1950s to early 1960s. The initial group of roads were all named after famous poets. For those unfamiliar with Felicia Hemans (1793-1835), she is most famous for the line 'The boy stood on the burning deck', from her poem 'Casabianca', written in the 19th century. In about 1812 or 1813 she lived in Daventry High Street when her husband was captain of the local militia. John Dryden, the first Poet Laureate (1658-1688) was cousin of Sir Robert Dryden, who lived in the locality at Canons Ashby. The estate was extended in the 1970s and is now known as The Headlands.

▶ **THE GREENWAY**
c1965 D83036

On the right of this
photograph is the first
Daventry bypass, dating
from about 1935. A new
bypass superseded it in the
1970s, when Daventry was
expanded. The houses in the
Greenway are 1960s infill
with their own service road.

◄ DANEHOLME ESTATE
c1965 D83056

This view looks west from the old Welton road across the Daneholme Estate at the point when the builder had run into financial difficulties and the development stopped. The estate was eventually finished a few years later, and now joins the Ashby and Welton Roads together.

▶ **THE FORD MOTOR COMPANY INTERNATIONAL DISTRIBUTION CENTRE**
c1965 D83086

Mr Frost, a local farmer, had to sell some of his land to allow Ford's to build their international distribution centre which opened in 1968. At that time it was one of the biggest warehouses in England; the staff came largely from their factories in Dagenham. They are still a major employer in Daventry.

◀ **FROM NEWNHAM HILL**
c1960 D83033

We are looking down on Daventry from Newnham Hill, a view that has been changed by a pink rash of housing estates as the town rapidly expanded from its comfortable 5000 in 1955 to around 25,000 in 2005. The projected maximum is 40,000! One 'building' that has disappeared is the gasometer, just visible on the left of the picture. With the advent of the natural gas supply grid, gasometers have become a rare feature in our townscapes.

▲ **FROM NEWNHAM HILL** *c1965* D83055

This is the same view as D83033, but five years later. The main difference is the appearance of Rex Arnold's factory, on the right, who made tubular steel furniture and car seat frames. Unfortunately, they have also closed down as the car industry has reformed itself. This was the start of the Long March industrial estate, which now extends far to the right and some way towards Newnham Hill.

◄ **BOROUGH HILL AND BBC DAVENTRY**
c1960 D83032

This view of Borough Hill was taken from neighbouring Newnham Hill. The forest of masts and aerials was a feature of the landscape for over 65 years. The first two were erected in 1925 when the BBC opened the first National Service from Daventry. This service was later transferred to Droitwich. The name of Daventry appeared with Paris, Hilversum and Berlin on the radio dials of the 20th century across the world.

◄ THE VIEW FROM
THE BRAUNSTON ROAD *c1960*
D83037

We are looking across the Headlands estate towards Borough Hill and the BBC masts. To the right the spire of Holy Church stands out above the centre of Daventry. The field in the view became British Timken's distribution depot for some years, but has now recently become another housing estate. British Timken came to Daventry and Northampton in 1954, and was one of the major employers for many years. Both the factories have recently closed, sad to say.

◀ **THE AERIALS AT BBC DAVENTRY**
c1965 D83082

This is the view that Daventrians saw of the BBC station. These masts are the result of the opening of the Empire Station in December 1932, in time for King George V to broadcast his Christmas message to all quarters of the Empire. This service, broadcasting round the clock in 40 languages, became well loved by 'ex pats', and it was a trusted source of truth and news both during the war and through the succeeding cold war. The service from Daventry was closed in 1991. We, in Daventry, still reminisce about hearing the World Service on toasters and kettles!

◀ **A CANAL TUNNEL** *c1955* D83014

The canal never arrived in Daventry, though there were plans to do so. This photo shows the Welton end of the Braunston Tunnel, built to connect the Grand Union Canal from London to the Oxford Canal at Braunston. The imposing house over the entrance was home to the tunnel keeper. In the 1920s Harry Webb was the occupant; with three colleagues, he carved a new pulpit for Welton church. The house has long since been demolished. The track up to the left was the route to Braunston for the horses while the narrow boats were 'legged' through the tunnel by the crew. This involved lying on a plank across the boats and using your feet on the tunnel sides to push the boats through the tunnel.

THE CANAL *c1965* D83042

Complementary to view D83014 on page 61, this was taken from the tunnel portal as a pair of working boats leave the Braunston Tunnel en route for London. Many of the 'butties', which are the unpowered towed boats, were originally horse-drawn. The two vessels moored on the right are British Waterways boats used to maintain the canal.

THE RESERVOIR *c1960* D83030

A chance for the local people to relax sailing on one of the canal reservoirs. These were built along the Grand Union Canal to maintain the water level in the canal. This one, on the Ashby Road, is still used by the Rugby and Daventry Sailing Club. The larger reservoir nearer to the town is now the centre of the country park.

DAVENTRY *from the air 1928* AF24681TL

THE VILLAGES

BRAUNSTON, *The Green c1955* B778007

Leaving Daventry northwards along the London to Holyhead turnpike, we arrive at Braunston, the hub of the canal network. From here you can travel to London, Birmingham, Leicester, Oxford and Stratford upon Avon by canal. At the top of the High Street stands the old National School, now the Village Hall (centre). After the new school was built in 1967, part of this building was used as a branch library for Braunston.

BRAUNSTON
The High Street
c1955 B778006

Looking west along the High Street, we see on the right the Dog and Gun, a Phipps public house, now closed and converted to a private house. Next door was the post office, recently demolished to allow restoration of the garden to a charming Georgian gentleman's house. The white house further on was the Crossed Guns, another public house. Behind the wall to the left was the Baptist Chapel of 1796, demolished in 1967.

BRAUNSTON, *The High Street c1950* B778004

As we move further west, we can identify the van on the left as a Mackeson Stout delivery van. Just beyond it, the half-timbered house is believed to be the oldest building in Braunston. Further down to the right was the village bakery with a 'Hovis' sign on the façade. This bakery was in business into the 1990s.

▶ **BRAUNSTON**
The Church c1955
B778001

All Saints' Church was built in 1849 to replace a crumbling medieval building. It was later re-ordered inside by William Butterfield, probably while he was working nearby at Rugby. The house to the right with a corrugated iron roof, now demolished, shows a common solution to failing thatch. Often the tin was put on over the remaining thatch- an inelegant but cost-effective solution to a leaking roof!

◀ **BRAUNSTON**
The Canal c1965 B778014

We are looking westwards along the Grand Union Canal on its way to Birmingham, at point where it originally joined the Oxford Canal. This junction was later moved further on, and the 'cut' to the left became the entrance to the 'pound'. The building on the left is the Stop House, where boats would stop to pay their tolls as they moved from one canal company canal to another. The 'Belmont' (centre left) is the butty to the 'Stanton' (next to it), belonging originally to Barlows. Butties were the un-powered boats towed by their powered partner.

▲ **BRAUNSTON,** *The Canal c1965* B778016

The 1960s was a turning point for the canals as the working boats' cargoes were switched to the roads, particularly the new M1 motorway. Many of the old boats were converted for cruising, but this one may well have been built to order. In the background is the A45 London to Holyhead turnpike. Just past this is the new Oxford Canal junction.

◄ **BRAUNSTON**
The Canal c1965 B778026

Blue Line, whose buildings and offices we see here, was a pioneer company in promoting canal cruising both here and in France. The buildings and covered dry dock are situated on the original route of the Oxford Canal. This was re-engineered around 1830, after the Grand Union Canal was built. The cut to the left leads to the pound, now the marina.

▶ BRAUNSTON
The Marina c1965
B778015

The marina was originally a reservoir to maintain levels in the Grand Union Canal; it was also used as a pound to moor working boats. Water was pumped from here up to the top lock. The line of bushes and trees in the middle distance hide the embankment of the railway line, which ran from Weedon through Daventry to Leamington. The service was withdrawn in 1959.

◀ NEWNHAM
Badby Road c1955 N251003

Newnham is situated south of Daventry, and is reached by a narrow country lane passing over Newnham Hill. On the top of the hill is the outer navigation station for Heathrow Airport, used by the Trans-Atlantic flights. This row of houses is still there today, but perhaps looking a little more looked-after. The gable-ended building in the distance has long since gone, and modern houses have been built on both sides of the Badby Road. The railings have also been removed, leaving a much more welcoming and open view of this charming village.

▲ **NEWNHAM,** *The Romer Arms c1955* N251012

This Edwardian building replaces an earlier private house. We are not sure when it became the 'local', but it is thought that Mr Romer Williams, whose name it preserves, was the resident of Newnham Hall for the first decades of the 20th century. It is not unreasonable to surmise that there is some connection with the rebuilding of this house. To the left was the Co-operative store, now the Village Stores. To the right the 'Lyons Tea' sign signifies another shop, of which no evidence could be found.

◀ **NEWNHAM**
School Hill c1955 N251006

Here we are looking up School Hill towards what was the New Inn, kept by Albert Howard, who started supplying fuel for the new motorcar, perhaps in addition to beer for the passengers. The petrol pumps were still in situ when Frith's photographer took this picture. The school, which is still flourishing, is on the right just round the bend - note the old 'torch of learning' school sign. The school opened on this site in 1915. It was built using timber from Russia.

▼ **NEWNHAM,** *The Cottage c1955* N251008

The delightful mid Victorian house on the right is built in Strawberry Hill Gothic style. The Cottage, as it is known, was built on the site of three cottages by the owner of the adjacent house. It was effectively a dower house, as the widow moved out from next door to allow the next generation to move in.

► **NEWNHAM**
St Michael's Church c1955 N251007

St Michael's Church is unique in the county in having the base of the tower open on three sides. There is a picture with the arches walled up, but they were unblocked in the mid 1800s. From then until 1940 the bell ringers operated in the open air! The tower was refurbished and the bells rehung in 1940. It is thought that it was at this time that the ringers moved indoors to the tower room. The war memorial on the right was consecrated in 1920.

NEWNHAM
Church Street c1955
N251010

Next door to the parish church is the Village Hall. This started life as a farmhouse, which was converted to a Poorhouse in 1783. When the Daventry Union Workhouse opened in 1834 (see D83067 page 47, Danetre Hospital) the building was converted into three cottages. 1877 saw further changes, as it became the village school until the building of the present school in 1915. It was rescued from decay by the Women's' Institute in 1932 to be used as a Village Hall, a function it carries on today.

NEWNHAM
The Village c1955
N251009

The photographer has now moved up to the parish church to catch this lovely village scene. The first building past the row of cottages on the left was the post office and a beer house many years ago. In the 1960s it was a village shop, but that now has closed. Further up is Crabtree Farm, built on the site of six burnt-out cottages in 1733. The two larger cottages this side of the old post office have been altered to form one private house.

▼ **STAVERTON,** *Daventry Road c1955* S557001

Leaving Daventry on the west-bound turnpike to Warwick and Stratford upon Avon we arrive at Staverton village. On the way to Staverton, in a lay-by is one of Telford's toll houses. When this photograph was taken there was a filling station opposite the New Inn. Today it is a car showroom. Someone has parked on the left to collect the new-laid eggs advertised on a roadside sign. With today's traffic, this would not be a wise place to stop, as this road can be very busy! The huge cedar tree towering over the 'New Laid Eggs' sign was blown down by a gale in the 1970s.

▶ **STAVERTON**
Daventry Road c1955
S557013

Having perhaps purchased some eggs, the photographer is now looking in the Southam direction along the road past the filling station. The house on the left is still there, but well hidden by trees now. The old coach house selling eggs is now a private house.

STAVERTON
The Old Crown
c1955 S557010

This is a view of the real centre of the village looking up Oakham Lane. It is sign of the times that the children were safe to play in the road, although Staverton still offers a fairly quiet environment with little traffic. The house in the picture is now a private house, but it was the Crown Inn until it closed in 1951 or 1952.

STAVERTON
The Village Pond
c1955 S557003

This view puts the old Crown Inn into context. The village pond, originally for watering horses, was filled in about 1960 and the area is now a pleasant village green, still with some of the original trees. To the right there is a pair of post war council houses, a typical development in most of our villages.

STAVERTON
Oakham Lane c1955
S557005

Oakham Lane is one of the streets leading from the village green. The building with the white window partially obscured behind the tree was the village school. The gap after the first house on the right hides the site where the Co-operative shop and the post office were. The shop has closed, and the post office is now run from a private house.

▶ **STAVERTON**
Croft Lane c1955 S557007

After fifty years, this view is largely unaltered. The small semi-circular extension on the cottage at the end of Croft Lane is a bread oven. The chimneys in the distance probably belong to The Croft, an interesting building still retaining some of its medieval character.

◄ STAVERTON
The Village Pond
c1955 S557009

Looking over the village pond we see on the right a building with a black door and shutter. This was the village bakehouse, where your Sunday joint would be cooked while you attended church. The low building next door has disappeared, and the adjacent cottage has been extended.

▶ **STAVERTON**
Manor Road c1955
S557004

We are looking west over the village pond into Manor Road; the house on the left is The Beeches. Needless to say, Manor Road leads to Staverton Manor and on up to The Croft, one of the oldest houses left in the village.

◀ **STAVERTON**
The Village and the Church c1955 S557012

Here we have a fine view of St Mary's Church from Church Street. The road crossing the picture from left to right immediately past the cottages on the left was the Daventry to Warwick turnpike and the main Warwick Road until the bypass was built in the 1990s. This allowed Staverton to regain a lot of its peaceful charm which had been destroyed by the motor car.

▲ **STAVERTON,** *The New Inn c1955* S557014

The New Inn, on the edge of the village, is on the Daventry to Warwick turnpike, and the name suggests it may have been opened because of the turnpike traffic. This was one of Phipps's houses; the Northampton brewers were taken over by Watney's in the 1960s. Today this pub sports the name of the Countryman.

◄ **LOWER WEEDON**
Church Street c1955 L582001

If we leave Daventry eastwards on the London turnpike, we arrive at Road Weedon, the portion of Weedon village on the main road. It is here that the turnpike rejoins the Roman road called Watling Street. This view along Church Street in Lower Weedon is little changed except for Cowie's general stores (centre), which was replaced by a modern mini-supermarket in the 1960s. The alleyway to the left used to lead to the Roman Catholic Church, before it was rebuilt in West Street behind the photographer.

▶ **ROAD WEEDON**
The New Inn c1965
R352009

The New Inn, sporting its new Watney's Red Barrel sign by the door and the sign board with the house style lettering, stands up the hill in Road Weedon on the old London to Holyhead turnpike. The inn is now called the Heart of England, and actually stands in the parish of Dodford. The boundary runs along the A45 and veers left by the Lawn Works to meet the A5, Watling Street.

◀ **ROAD WEEDON**
Jan's Folly c1965
R352013

Jan's Folly stands at the junction of the A45 and A5 trunk road. It was originally one of Telford's tollhouses on the London to Holyhead turnpike. It was renamed the Crossroads Hotel when the house to the left was demolished and the hotel expanded, sporting a fine clock tower. Besides offering 'All Day Catering', Jan's Folly also sold antiques, a trade still important to Weedon.

▲ **ROAD WEEDON,** *The Globe Hotel c1965* R352015

As we look down to the junction with Watling Street, on the left is the former W H Smith's shop, now offering haircuts! The Globe Hotel next door is still in business; originally it had a pleasant garden in front. Below it was yet another inn, the White Hart. The building to the right was George Green's smithy, and is now the site of the A45 for Northampton.

◀ **ROAD WEEDON**
The Globe Hotel c1955
R352303

This was taken about ten years earlier than photograph W593015, and the Globe Hotel has yet to acquire the extension. You can also see the National Benzole filling station in the hotel car park. The first garage in Weedon was opposite the Globe Hotel in the Wheatsheaf car park. Just on the edge of the photograph (right) is George Green's smithy, demolished during road improvements in the 1970s.

ROAD WEEDON
Watling Street c1955
R352014

The photographer is now looking south along Watling Street back to Road Weedon. To the right are the post-war council houses and the filling station in the Globe Hotel car park. The blue sign for the M1 (left) is a new addition to the countryside. The design for these signs was decided in 1962, three years after the M1 opened.

WELTON, *St Martin's Church c1955* W477003

Welton lies to the north of Daventry, originally along a country lane. Expansion has altered much of this lane, as it now runs along the edge of the Lang Farm estate. St Martin's Church is a good solid medieval building, though we are lucky it is still here: there was a disastrous fire in the 19th century, which destroyed the roof. Fortunately, it was rebuilt, and through the connections of Mr Clarke of Welton Place with the Tsar of Russia, the sanctuary is paved with pieces of malachite. Mr Clarke was the Tsar's advisor on rice farming.

WELTON
High Street c1955
W477004

This view of Welton, looking back up the main street, has changed dramatically in recent years. The gabled building to the right was the Village Hall, replaced in the early 1960s by the present hall. Beyond is the White Horse, still in business, though the Northampton Brewery, with its NBC Star trademark, has long since passed into history. The cottages on the left have been partially replaced by new large houses.

WELTON, *High Street c1955* W477005

Here we have a close up view of the White Horse and a good view of the old Village Hall, where WI meetings had to be fairly restrained in case the floor gave way! The new hall was built with a generous donation from Lady and Sir Halford Reddish, director of Rugby Cement. Modern detached houses have replaced some of the cottages on the far right.

WELTON, *High Street c1955* W477010a

This view down the main street has changed little over the years. The whitewashed pub, the White Horse, is still there, and so is the church. The smithy on left has gone as its trade diminished. The Gilbert Scott phone box has been replaced with a modern sleek aluminium one, and some of the cottages in the distance have been modernised.

WELTON, *The Crossroads c1955* W477008

This is a bit of a misnomer, as it is only a T-junction – but the view is virtually unchanged today. It is on the top edge of the village: the road to the left leads out of the village towards Watling Street, and the one to the right takes you into the village street.

BIBLIOGRAPHY

Brown, A E	**Early Daventry**	Leicester University	1991	ISBN 0-90150-744-X
Greenall, R L	**Daventry Past**	Phillimore	1999	ISBN 1-86077-108-4
Hornby, S (compiler)	**Daventry**	Tempus	1998	ISBN 0-75241-069-5

NAMES OF PRE-PUBLICATION BUYERS

The following people have kindly supported this book by subscribing to copies before publication.

Mrs A E Agius, Daventry and Mr C J Agius, Daventry

The Altimas Family, Daventry

In memory of David Paul Ashfield

Mr & Mrs M W F Ayers

In memory of Arthur & Ethel Bacon

J & D Barker, Hillside Road, Flore

Frank E S Barnstable

John Bass & Family, Daventry

J D Baxter, Badby, Daventry, NN11 3AR

Jan Beasley

'My childhood memories', Jennifer Benjamin

In fond memory of Margaret Berry 2005

In memory of H J Bilverstone

Stuart & Mali Birt & their family 2005

The Boans Family, Daventry

The Bond Family, Daventry

Mr & Mrs D & S Brewer, Daventry

Mr & Mrs Robert Maitland Brown

John & Jane Buckley, Daventry

The Bunn Family of Braunston

M P Carwardine, Daventry

Christopher Chambers of Welton

Mr Derek & Mrs Irene Clarke, formerly of Daventry

Robert William Clarke

In memory of William & Annie Clarke

In memory of K G & M Clarke, Daventry

Graham Claxton

Mr M J & Mrs L T Claydon

Daniel I Coles, Badby

Josephine Collins

Property of Pete Cotton, Daventry

B J Coward, and in memory of Mrs Y Coward

Mr & Mrs J G Coward & Family, Danetre

In memory of the Cox, Wilson & Todd Families

The Curtis Family, Daventry

John & Kath Dark, Staverton

Colin & Philippa Davenport

Jonathan Davenport

Daventry Express

Councillor G Edwards Davidson

The Davis Family, Daventry

Paddy Davis, Janet Western, Daventry

Jim & Lynn Davis, Daventry

The Dodd Family, Daventry

Mr & Mrs D A Dymott, Daventry

Joyce Lilian Eaton

The Emery Family, Daventry

The Engall Family

Vera England - Mothers Day 6 March 2005

As a tribute to Ron & May Fennell

The Finch Family, Daventry

In memory of Grace Flavell (nee Spence)

Robert A Franks, The Larches

To Mum & Dad, Mr & Mrs C Gay, Daventry

Peter & Chris Grossart, Braunston

In memory of Charles & Molly Hadlow

The Hagen Family, Daventry

George Halford

Mrs B A Hall, Newnham

In memory of John A Hall, Newnham

Mary & Cliff Harford & Family

Andrew Hartshorn on his birthday

Vicki Haynes

The Hesketh Family, Daventry

Mr & Mrs B J Hibbert, Daventry

Richard & Ena Hipwell

Albert Hodgkins & Margaret Hodgkins

Val Hopson

H A Hughes, Freeman of the Borough 1966

Mrs M A Hughes, Braunston

Colin & Geraldine Isom, Daventry

Jessie & Reg Jeffs & Family, Daventry

The Jennings Family, Daventry

'Memories of home', Caroline Jones, America

In memory of Gertie & Sid Kennell

Geoff & Carole Kenning, Pattishall

Wesley & Maureen Kenworthy, Daventry

The Kilner Family, Daventry

Joyce Elizabeth Kitchener

Eileen Lattaway, Daventry

The Lentons, Daneholm Cottages from 1938

The Lockland Family, Daventry
Tim Lownes, Flore
In memory of A G McKendrick, Northants
Hugh McPherson, Bishop, Daventry
The MacDonnell Family, Daventry
The Mason Family, Daventry
Hugh & Judi Mayes, Weltonfield
R & G McBean, Welton, Daventry
Brenda J & Robert P Mills, Daventry
Helen A Monaghan, born in Daventry 1976
The Morris Family, Braunston
Mr Francis R Morris & Mrs Lucy D Morris
Janet Morris, In memory of Eric A Morris
The Murray Family, Daventry
The Newman Family of Badby Road, Daventry
The Nightingale Family
Mr P W & Mrs B J Oliver, Daventry
In memory of P.S.294 T.C.S. Page, Daventry
David & Barbara Palmer, Daventry
Mr & Mrs R Payler, Kislingbury
Mr & Mrs Malcolm H Payne & Family
David Payne
J Payne
Andrew Pearson, Daventry, on his birthday
Nigel Pearson and son Lewis, Daventry
Tim Pearson, for his 70th birthday, 05/01/06
Dr C Perry & Mrs E Perry, Weedon
Ken & Betty Pettitt, Daventry
Mr T M Pitt & Mrs C A Pitt
Dr D P B & Mrs J F Pound, Charwelton
The Quinney Family, Daventry
The Raybould Family, Daventry
The Rayment Family, Daventry
The Read Family 2005
In memory of Les A Renshaw of Braunston
Ken & Doreen Ridley, Daventry
Jo, Graham, Eric Ridley, NSW, Australia
Betty Ridley, in loving memory of Stanley
Larry Roberts, Daventry
Mr H C Sargeant, 'Butcher', Sheaf Street
Scott Savage, Ashby Gate, Timken
Pete & Mary Scott from Mich & Mark
Peter Scott with love 2005

Nancy Newbery Scrutton, Newnham, Daventry
Michael Sergeant, Daventry
In memory of Ted & Sheila Sharpe 2005
Walter H Sheppard
John W Shortland, Weedon
Fond memories of Martin Shucksmith
Mr A & Mrs M Sims, Daventry and Weedon
Jennifer Smith, Daventry
John M Smith, Flore
As a tribute to Rudi Smith & Family, Daventry
Michael & Christine Smythe
Michael F Spence, Daventry
Mr A C & Mrs J T Stait of Daventry
'Memories of home', Katrina Stait, Daventry
Irene Stockil
Mr A H & Mrs S R Tate & Family, Daventry
Ashley J P Taylor, Crick
Celina J S Taylor, Crick
Mr D & Mrs P Taylor, Daventry
The Taylor Family, Crick
Mary & Arthur Taylor, Golden Wedding
    Anniversary 05/03/05
The Thompson Family, Welton
Mr G J Thompson & Mrs M E Thompson
Andrew Thomson & Family, Lang Farm
A W Tooby & L G Tooby, Daventry
Don & Pat Tooby, Wanganui, New Zealand
In memory of Sidney & Phyllis Trott
Stephen Turner
Peter & Alison Walls, Welton
John A Wattam, Long Buckby
The Webster Family, Daventry
Mrs M West, the Begley Family, Daventry
M J White, Daventry
In memory of our daughter, Claire Whyles
Jane Wilkins
Mr B & Mrs S J Williams, Daventry
Mr R & Mrs P G Williams, Daventry
In memory of F W S Wilson, Daventry
J D Worthington, Daventry
Glad & Eric Wylde, Golden Wedding 26 Feb 2005
Bob & Sonja Young, Daventry

INDEX

FREE PRINT OF YOUR CHOICE

Mounted Print
Overall size 14 x 11 inches (355 x 280mm)

Choose any Frith photograph in this book.
Simply complete the Voucher opposite and return it with your remittance for £2.25 (to cover postage and handling) and we will print the photograph of your choice in SEPIA (size 11 x 8 inches) and supply it in a cream mount with a burgundy rule line (overall size 14 x 11 inches).
Please note: photographs with a reference number starting with a "Z" are not Frith photographs and cannot be supplied under this offer.
Offer valid for delivery to one UK address only.

PLUS: **Order additional Mounted Prints at HALF PRICE - £7.49 each** (normally £14.99)
If you would like to order more Frith prints from this book, possibly as gifts for friends and family, you can buy them at half price (with no additional postage and handling costs).

PLUS: **Have your Mounted Prints framed**
For an extra £14.95 per print you can have your mounted print(s) framed in an elegant polished wood and gilt moulding, overall size 16 x 13 inches (no additional postage and handling required).

IMPORTANT!

These special prices are only available if you use this form to order . You must use the ORIGINAL VOUCHER on this page (no copies permitted). We can only despatch to one UK address. This offer cannot be combined with any other offer.

Send completed Voucher form to:
The Francis Frith Collection, Frith's Barn, Teffont, Salisbury, Wiltshire SP3 5QP

CHOOSE A PHOTOGRAPH FROM THIS BOOK

Voucher *for* **FREE** *and Reduced Price Frith Prints*

Please do not photocopy this voucher. Only the original is valid, so please fill it in, cut it out and return it to us with your order.

Picture ref no	Page no	Qty	Mounted @ £7.49	Framed + £14.95	Total Cost £
		1	Free of charge*	£	£
			£7.49	£	£
			£7.49	£	£
			£7.49	£	£
			£7.49	£	£
			£7.49	£	£

Please allow 28 days for delivery. Offer available to one UK address only

* Post & handling	£2.25
Total Order Cost	£

Title of this book . . . .

I enclose a cheque/postal order for £ . . . .
made payable to 'The Francis Frith Collection'

OR please debit my Mastercard / Visa / Maestro / Amex card, details below

Card Number

Issue No (Maestro only)   Valid from (Maestro)

Expires   Signature

Name Mr/Mrs/Ms . . . .
Address . . . .
. . . .
. . . .
. . . . Postcode . . . .
Daytime Tel No . . . .
Email . . . .

ISBN: 1-85937-670-3   Valid to 31/12/07

Free Print – see overleaf

Would you like to find out more about Francis Frith?

We have recently recruited some entertaining speakers who are happy to visit local groups, clubs and societies to give an illustrated talk documenting Frith's travels and photographs. If you are a member of such a group and are interested in hosting a presentation, we would love to hear from you.

Our speakers bring with them a small selection of our local town and county books, together with sample prints. They are happy to take orders. A small proportion of the order value is donated to the group who have hosted the presentation. The talks are therefore an excellent way of fundraising for small groups and societies.

Can you help us with information about any of the Frith photographs in this book?

We are gradually compiling an historical record for each of the photographs in the Frith archive. It is always fascinating to find out the names of the people shown in the pictures, as well as insights into the shops, buildings and other features depicted.

If you recognize anyone in the photographs in this book, or if you have information not already included in the author's caption, do let us know. We would love to hear from you, and will try to publish it in future books or articles.

Our production team

Frith books are produced by a small dedicated team at offices in the converted Grade II listed 18th-century barn at Teffont near Salisbury, illustrated above. Most have worked with the Frith Collection for many years. All have in common one quality: they have a passion for the Frith Collection. The team is constantly expanding, but currently includes:

Paul Baron, Phillip Brennan, Jason Buck, John Buck, Ruth Butler, Heather Crisp, David Davies, Louis du Mont, Isobel Hall, Lucy Hart, Julian Hight, Peter Horne, James Kinnear, Karen Kinnear, Tina Leary, Stuart Login, David Marsh, Sue Molloy, Glenda Morgan, Wayne Morgan, Sarah Roberts, Kate Rotondetto, Dean Scource, Eliza Sackett, Terence Sackett, Sandra Sampson, Adrian Sanders, Sandra Sanger, Julia Skinner, Miles Smith, Lewis Taylor, Shelley Tolcher, Lorraine Tuck, David Turner, Amanita Wainwright and Ricky Williams.